By Larry Davis

illustrated by Don Greer

squadron/signal publications

ISBN 0-89747-135-0

If you have any photographs of the aircraft, armor, soldiers or ships of any nation, particularly wartime snapshots, why not share them with us and help make Squadron/Signal's books all the more interesting and complete in the future. Any photograph sent to us will be copied and the original returned. The donor will be fully credited for any photos used. Please send them to: Squadron/Signal Publications, Inc., 1115 Crowley Dr., Carrollton, TX 75006.

List of Contributors

Air Force Museum
Gene Boswell
John Dienst
Jeff Ethell
Don Garrett
Fred LePage
Dave Menard
North American Aviation
Merle Olmsted
Warren Thompson
United States Air Force
Richard L. Ward

Looking every bit as sleek as the designers intended, the XP-51 displays the standard markings on US Army Air Corps aircraft prior to US involvement in World War II—red, white and blue rudder stripes; white star in a blue circle with a red center insignia on both wings, upper and lower; and 'U.S. ARMY' in black on the underside of the wing. (NAA)

Production Mustang III in delivery paint scheme of RAF Dark Green/Ocean Grey camouflage, with red outlined US star and bars insignia. The underside is Medium Sea Grey. (NAA)

Typhoon McGoon **from the 363rd FSq/357th FGp displaying the complete set of white friendly aircraft ID stripes on the nose, wings, horizontal and vertical tail. The code letters are in grey and the national insignia has been toned down with grey paint. (LePage)**

On 8 March 1945, RAF Mustangs were ordered to remove all camouflage paint. This of course included any leftover D-Day stripes. RAF Mustangs in natural metal finish retained all the *standard* markings as on camouflage aircraft except that code letters were in black. Anti-glare panels were in flat Olive Drab.

The US Army Air Corps began receiving production P-51 Mustangs in 1942. Initially some were delivered in the British Dark Green/Dark Earth/Sky camouflage scheme. These however were the exception of the rule. Except for those early few, most were delivered in the standard Army Air Force camouflage of Olive Drab (34087) upper surfaces, and Neutral Grey (36173) undersides. P-51 Mustangs had 40 inch 'star-in-circle' cocardes with the red ball in the center. Wing insignia was the same but only 35 inches in size. On both sides of the aft fuselage was a 10 inch high, six digit radio call number in Identification Yellow (33538). P-51As and A-36As were identical except for a 30 inch fuselage cocarde. The red 'meatball' was dropped from the insignia in August 1942 - **something to do with trigger-happy gunners in the Pacific shooting at anything resembling a Japanese 'meatball'.** Cocardes of Britain and North Africa based aircraft were trimmed with a two inch wide ID Yellow ring.

The North Africa based Mustangs also adopted the 12 inch wing ID bands as seen on RAF Mustang Is. Some even had US flags painted on the vertical tail surface. Unit codes were at first applied in white, directly over the radio call number. In June 1943 the bars were added to the national insignia and a two inch red trim line bordered the entire national insignia. A blue border replaced the red in September 1943. Addition of the bars to the national insignia forced Army Air Force personnel to move the radio call number onto the vertical tail. The size was cut down to 8 inches in height but remained yellow in color.

P-51Bs began arriving in England during September 1943. Their finish was identical to previous Army Air Force P-51s. ID stripes, very similar to RAF Mustangs, were applied in November 1943 and consisted of a white spinner and 12 inch white band on the nose, 12 inch bands on both sides of the vertical tail, and 15 inch stripes around both upper and lower wing and horizontal tail surfaces. The tail stripes **could** be removed after March 1944. Standard unit codes were a two letter squadron code forward of the national insignia on the fuselage, and a single letter *plane-in-squadron* code aft of the star and bar - all in white. The radio call number was on the vertical tail, 8 inches high and yellow in color.

Natural metal finish Mustangs began to appear with the 770th P-51B and 201st P-51C. This would be the standard finish for all Mustangs from this point on. One of the little known facts is that natural metal Mustangs weren't all 'natural metal'! The entire upper and lower main wing, from root to wingtip, excluding flaps and ailerons, was first primed with chromate yellow, then **painted** gloss silver. It was done to all natural metal P-51B, C, D and K aircraft to help smooth the airflow over the wing. This, of course, deteriorated rapidly and usually was stripped off and the wing polished and waxed to a smooth finish. Unit ID codes were the same style and type as on camouflage aircraft except the color was now Black (37038). Many units also outlined the code letters in the group or squadron color. Aircraft ID stripes on the wings were changed from white to black. The ID bands on both the nose and tail surfaces were deleted.

On 4 June 1944 the famous D-Day Invasion Stripes were applied to all tactical aircraft of the 8th and 9th Air Forces. The bands, alternate 18 inch wide black and white stripes, were applied to both camouflage and natural metal aircraft. They were identical to RAF Invasion Stripes except for location. The fuselage bands were centered on the star in the national insignia, while the wing stripes began at a point 8 inches inboard of the outer edge of the flap. Most of the stripes were hastily hand painted, without masking, and were very ragged in appearance. In July 1944, with the invasion beaches secured, Fighter Command ordered the removal of all *upper* surface stripes. By September 1944, only the lower fuselage stripes remained. In December 1944, all remnants of the D-Day stripes were ordered removed.

It's D-Day and all tactical aircraft are ordered to carry alternate white and black friendly aircraft recognition bands around the wings and fuselage. Here is the 376th FSq, configured with long range tanks for bomber escort, taxiing for takeoff with a mixture of natural metal and camouflaged aircraft. The camouflaged machine left of center carries white code letters. (USAF)

(Below) In July 1944, with US aircraft in place on European airfields, Fighter Command ordered all D-Day stripes removed from upper surfaces. The stripes were very hastily put on and they were even more hastily covered up with a brush full of Olive Drab. C3☆A is from the 382nd FSq/363rd FGp, one of the first units to land on the continent. Notice how the paint is peeling, especially on the tail surfaces. (USAF)

Leakin' Liz from the 358th FSq/355th FGp in full D-Day stripes. The stripes were hastily, and usually crudely, applied both with a brush and by spray gun. Note the rear view mirror attached to the windscreen. (355th FGp Assn via Ethell)

(Below) A flight of four aircraft from the 374th FSq/361st FGp enroute to a target in Germany. The B models have overpainted their D-Day stripes with Olive Drab while the P-51Ds have had their stripes painted over with silver. *Bald Eagle,* B7☆E carries blue and yellow stripes below the antiglare panel, which is Olive Drab, and on the wingtips and rudder trim. *Tika,* B7☆R, has blue wing, tail and stabilizer tips. All aircraft have yellow spinners and 12 inches of the nose. (USAF)

A sharkmouthed P-51C from the 26th FSq, 51st FGp in China. All painted surfaces suffered from the China weather and poor field maintenance - no fault of the ground crews. The tail stripes, which are repeated on both stabilizers, are yellow with black trim. Number '261' is in white. The spinner and wingtips are in yellow. (USAF)

(Below) Another Mustang III, this time from No. 64 Squadron. The plane-in-squadron code letter H has been painted over the serial number and Sky band on the aft fuselage. All fuselage codes are in white. Note that the in-squadron code H has been repeated on a small black circle on each outer landing gear door. (Smith via Ethell)

Squadron Leader D.F. Westrena, CO of No. 65 Squadron, RNZAF, flew this Mustang III to victory over eleven Germans. The code letters and aft fuselage band are Sky. All other stripes are white. The spinner is red. (Smith via Ethell)

(Below) *Maggie's Drawers,* from the 380th FSq, 363rd FGp, over England prior to D-Day. The national insignia has been greyed out to reduce the chances of a Luftwaffe pilot using the white star and bar as a sighting device. (USAF)

The 353rd FGp used this P-51C as a hack for command meetings or other non-combat jaunts around England. The aircraft, although 'war weary', meaning a high-time airframe, was highly maintained as were most ETO Mustangs. The 'Malcolm hood', a bubble canopy for razorback Mustangs, can be clearly seen. (USAF)

Along with the D-Day stripes came a 'suggestion' from 8th Fighter Command that units return to camouflage paint. The thinking was that since the units would be operating from forward airfields on the continent, camouflage paint might hide some aircraft from expected Luftwaffe air attacks. It would also hide ground attack aircraft from the prying eyes of defending Luftwaffe pilots looking for an easy kill. Camouflage colors and patterns were left entirely up to the units. Thus it was not unusual to have one unit, such as the 357th FGp, in full camouflage of Olive Drab or Medium Green (34092) upper surfaces, with Light Grey, Neutral Grey, or Sky undersurfaces; while a unit such as the 343rd Fighter Squadron, in the 55th Group, painted only the fuselage in Olive Drab, and this was more artistic than functional. The 361st Fighter Group camouflaged some of their aircraft in Insignia Blue. Some units such as the 4th Fighter Group, disdained the use of camouflage entirely. By December 1944, camouflage was being removed from most aircraft in favor of polished metal for greater speed - camouflaged aircraft suffered a loss of about 20MPH top speed.

Interior paint details for Mustangs have not changed much over the years whether in service with the RAF, USAAF, USAF, or other nations. Cockpits have been painted Interior or Chromate Green (24151) with natural metal bucket seats. Exceptions to this are some Korean War F-51Ds which had Black cockpit walls. Most Mustangs rebuilt for foreign service after 1955 have Aircraft Grey (36473) cockpits. Engine bays and other compartment interiors can be found in either Chromate Yellow (33481) or Chromate Green. Main wheel wells and landing gear doors are in silver paint, with the rear wall of the gear bay being in Chromate Yellow or Green as this is part of the wing main spar. Antiglare panels were usually Olive Drab but Black was very common in Korea. Stenciling, no matter what type of exterior finish, was in Black.

F-82 Twin Mustangs came in two finishes—natural metal for training aircraft and Day Fighter/Long Range Escort aircraft; and Gloss Black on night fighters. Natural metal aircraft were finished exactly the same as their single-engine cousins, with black lettering and stencil information. Night fighter F-82F/G/H aircraft had Insignia Red buzz and serial numbers, plus the 'USAF' on upper right and lower left wings. In addition, the blue was deleted from the national insignia. Cockpit interiors were in Interior Green, while landing gear bays and door interiors were in silver.

The Mustang was rapidly phased out of active US Air Force service following a brief comeback as a front line aircraft during the Korean War. But she was to soldier on with many other air forces around the world. Service with Israel and many Latin American air forces would see a return to camouflage - in so many different patterns and colors that another book would be needed to cover them all. But no matter what the country's flag they flew under, nor what finish they wore, the Mustang was still *The most aerodynamically perfect pursuit plane in existance.*

When the war ended, many P-51s were bought by ex-GIs or other civilians, and used for racing. Glenn McCarthy's very colorful ***Latin American Special*** **was one of the many P-51s used in this manner.**

P-51A Mustang

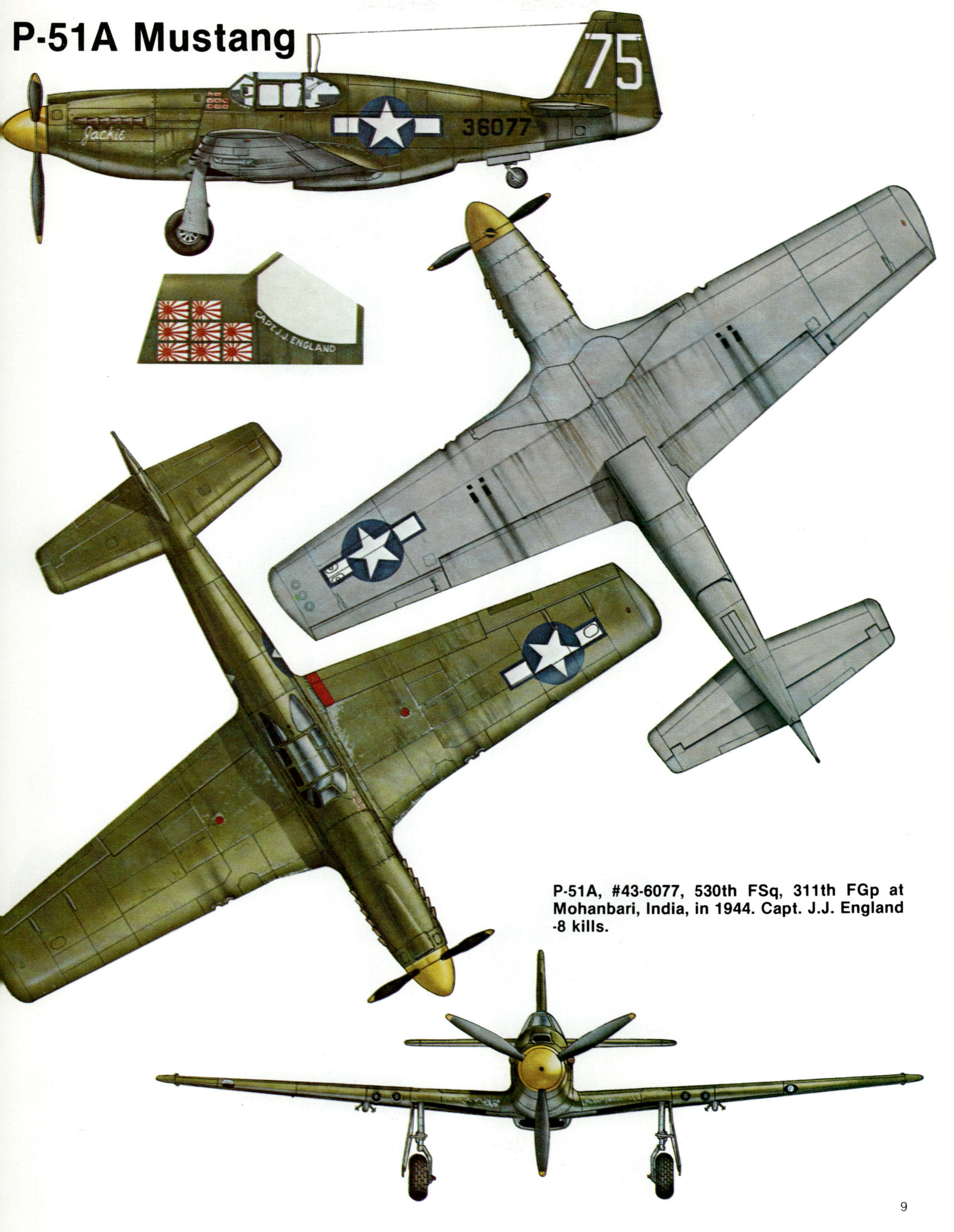

P-51A, #43-6077, 530th FSq, 311th FGp at Mohanbari, India, in 1944. Capt. J.J. England -8 kills.

P-51A Details

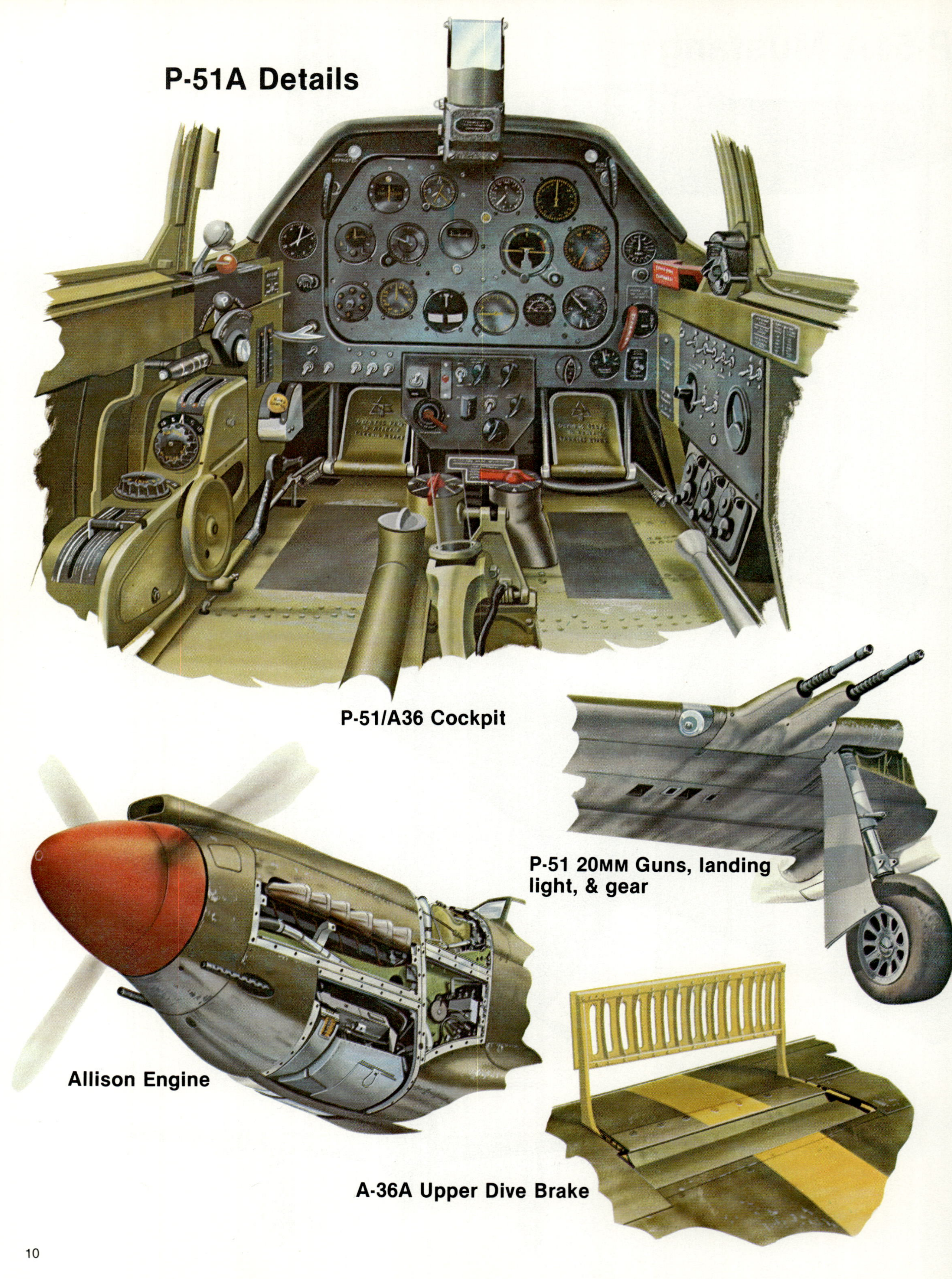

P-51/A36 Cockpit

P-51 20MM Guns, landing light, & gear

Allison Engine

A-36A Upper Dive Brake

P-51A

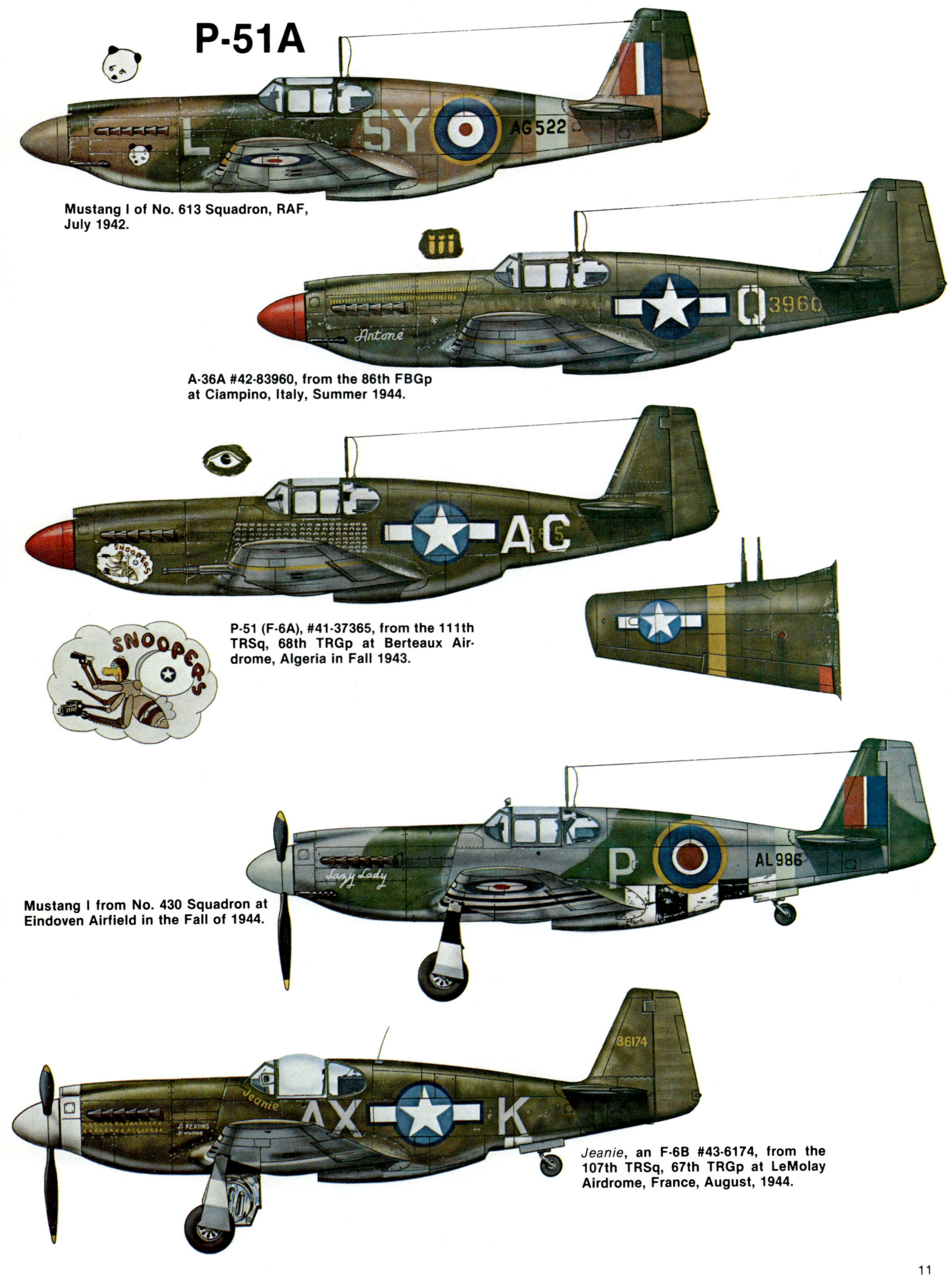

Mustang I of No. 613 Squadron, RAF, July 1942.

A-36A #42-83960, from the 86th FBGp at Ciampino, Italy, Summer 1944.

P-51 (F-6A), #41-37365, from the 111th TRSq, 68th TRGp at Berteaux Airdrome, Algeria in Fall 1943.

Mustang I from No. 430 Squadron at Eindoven Airfield in the Fall of 1944.

Jeanie, an F-6B #43-6174, from the 107th TRSq, 67th TRGp at LeMolay Airdrome, France, August, 1944.

P-51B

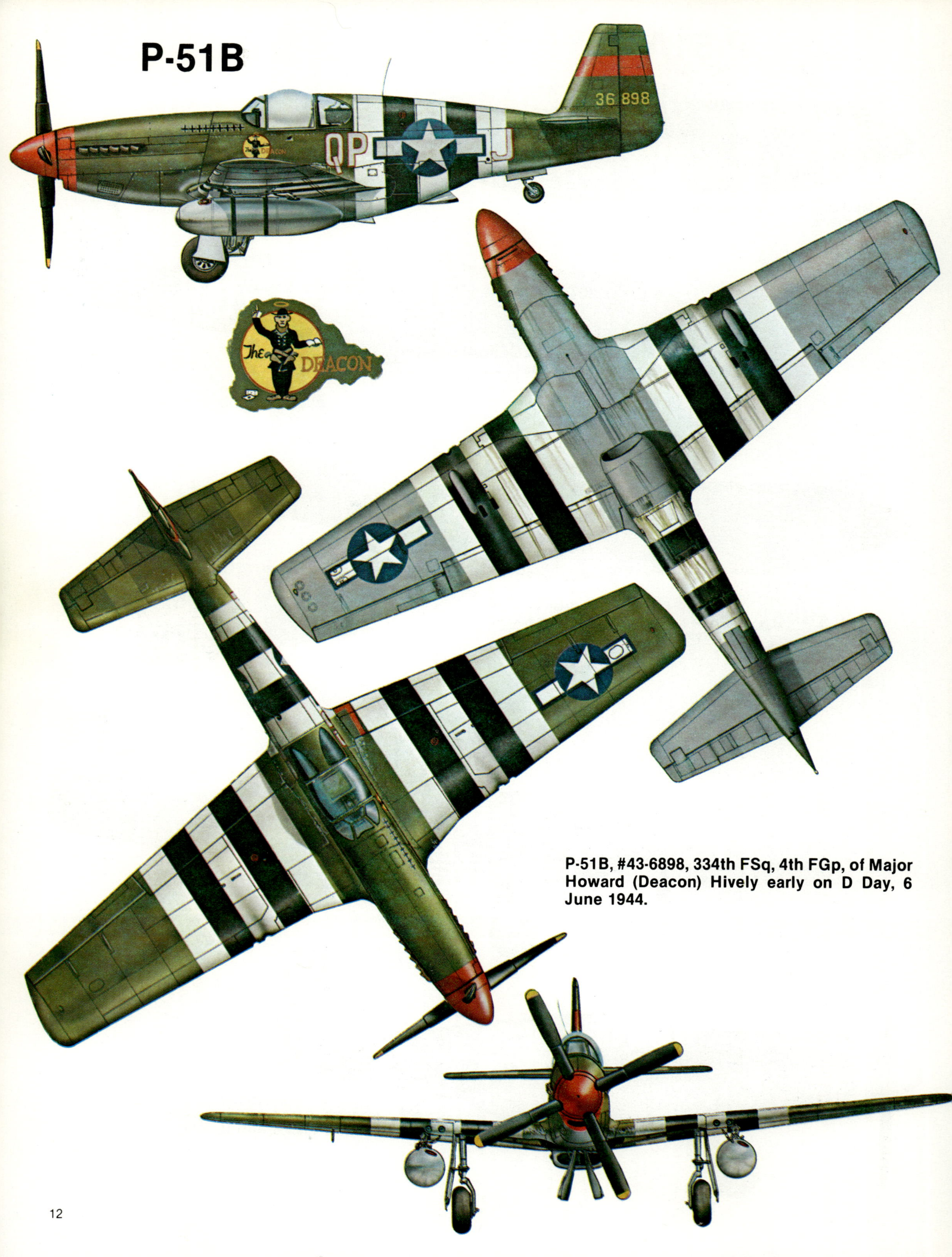

P-51B, #43-6898, 334th FSq, 4th FGp, of Major Howard (Deacon) Hively early on D Day, 6 June 1944.

P-51B Details

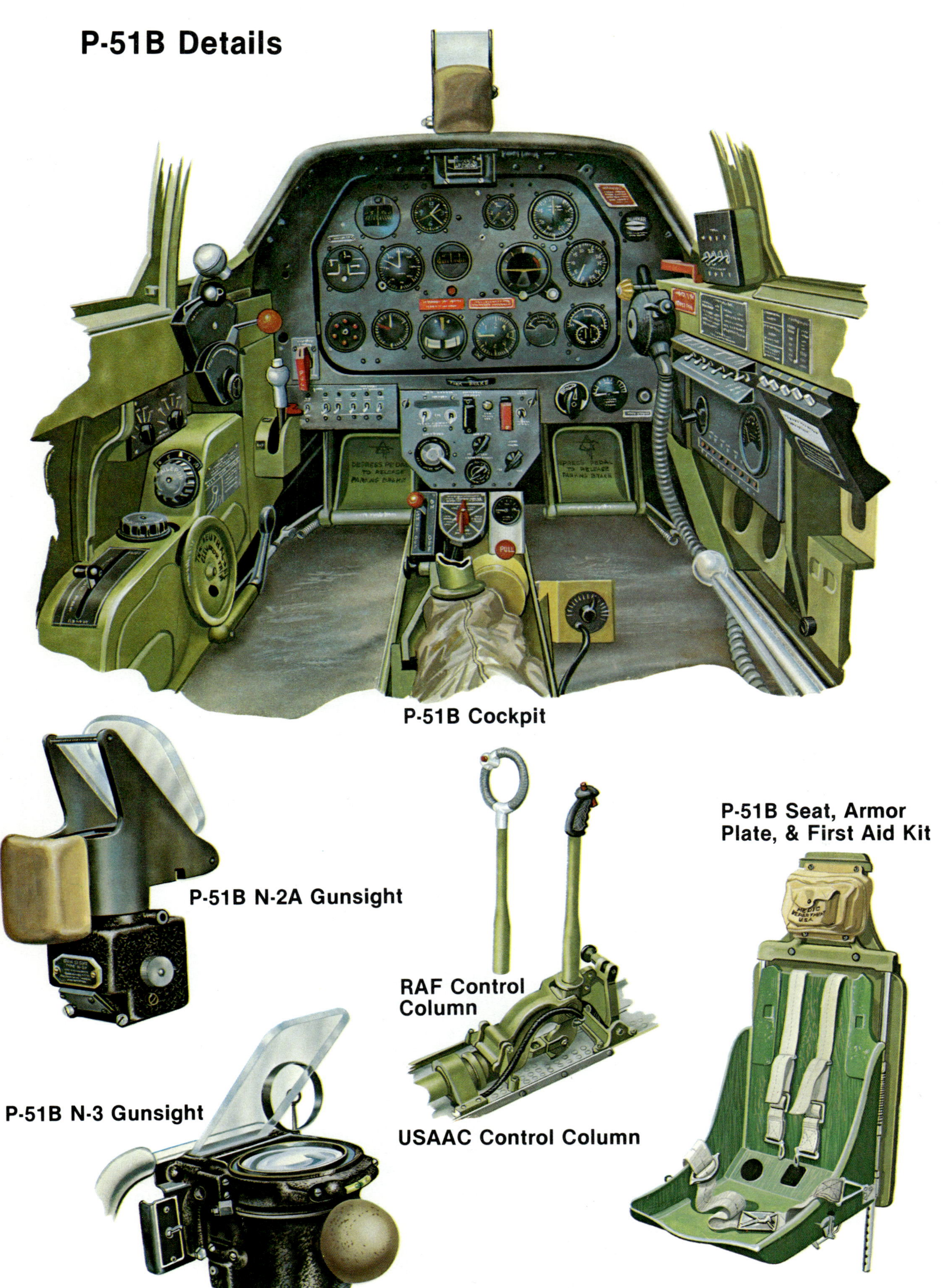

P-51B Cockpit

P-51B N-2A Gunsight

P-51B N-3 Gunsight

RAF Control Column

USAAC Control Column

P-51B Seat, Armor Plate, & First Aid Kit

P-51B Details

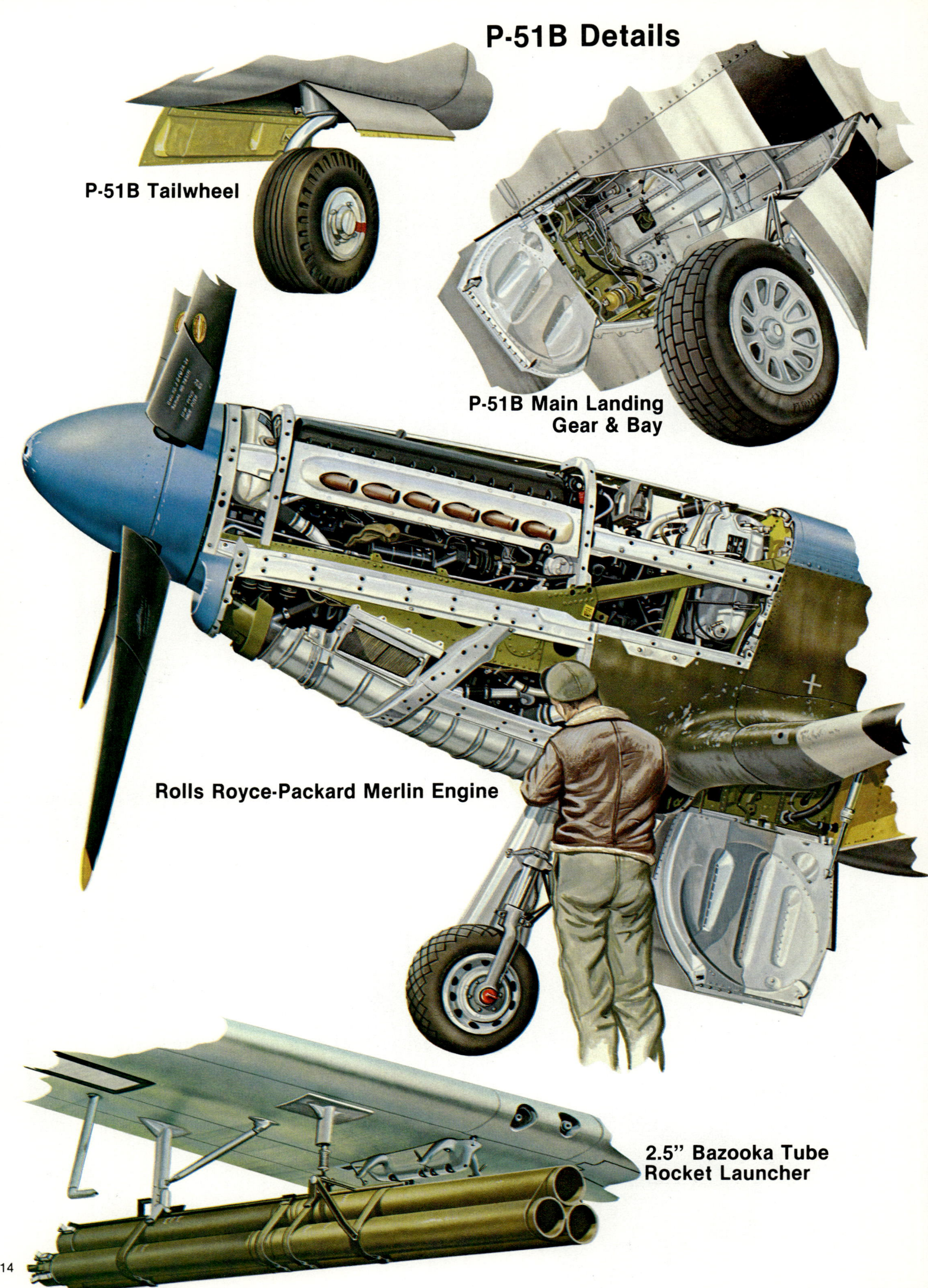

P-51B Details

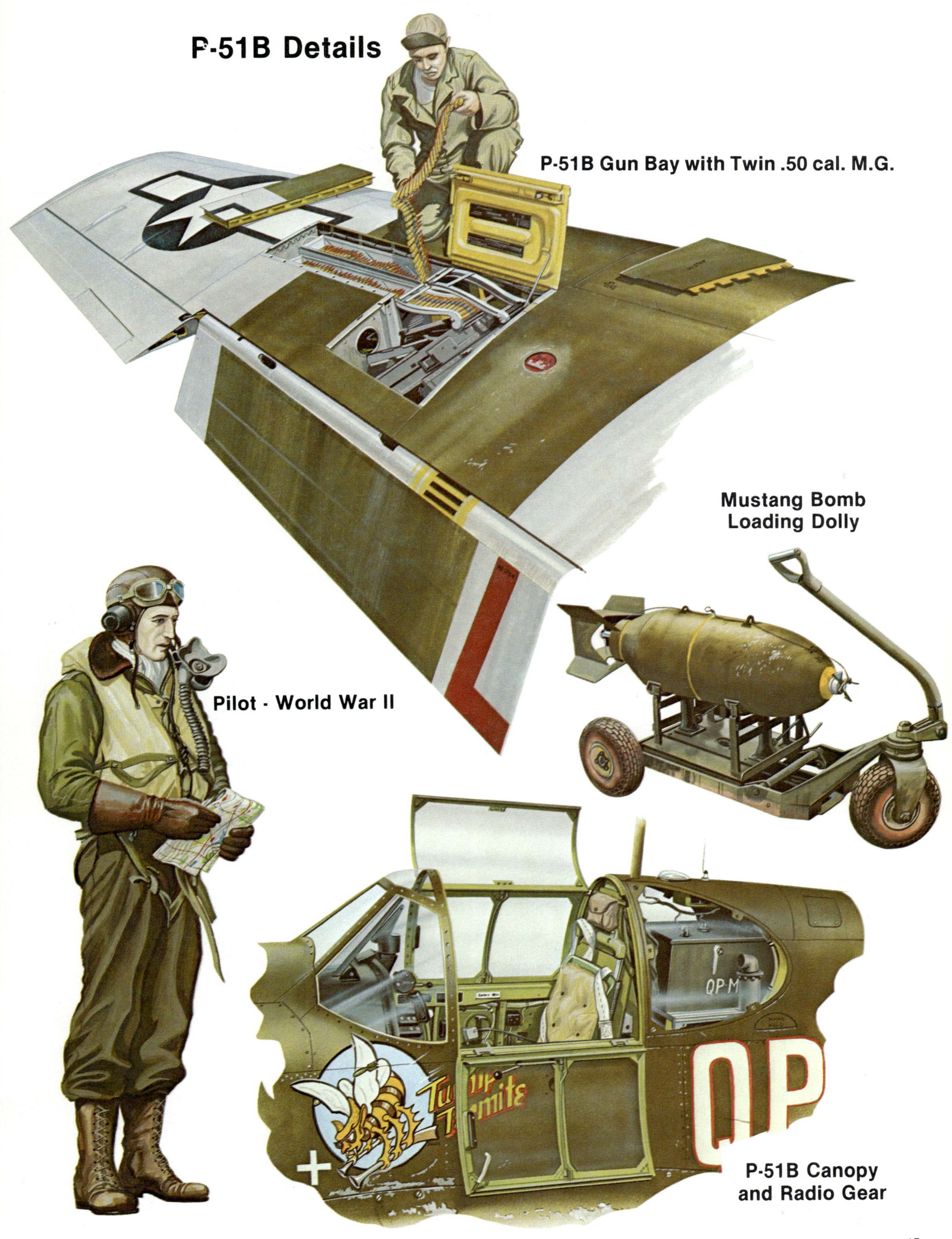

P-51B Gun Bay with Twin .50 cal. M.G.

Mustang Bomb Loading Dolly

Pilot - World War II

P-51B Canopy and Radio Gear

P-51B

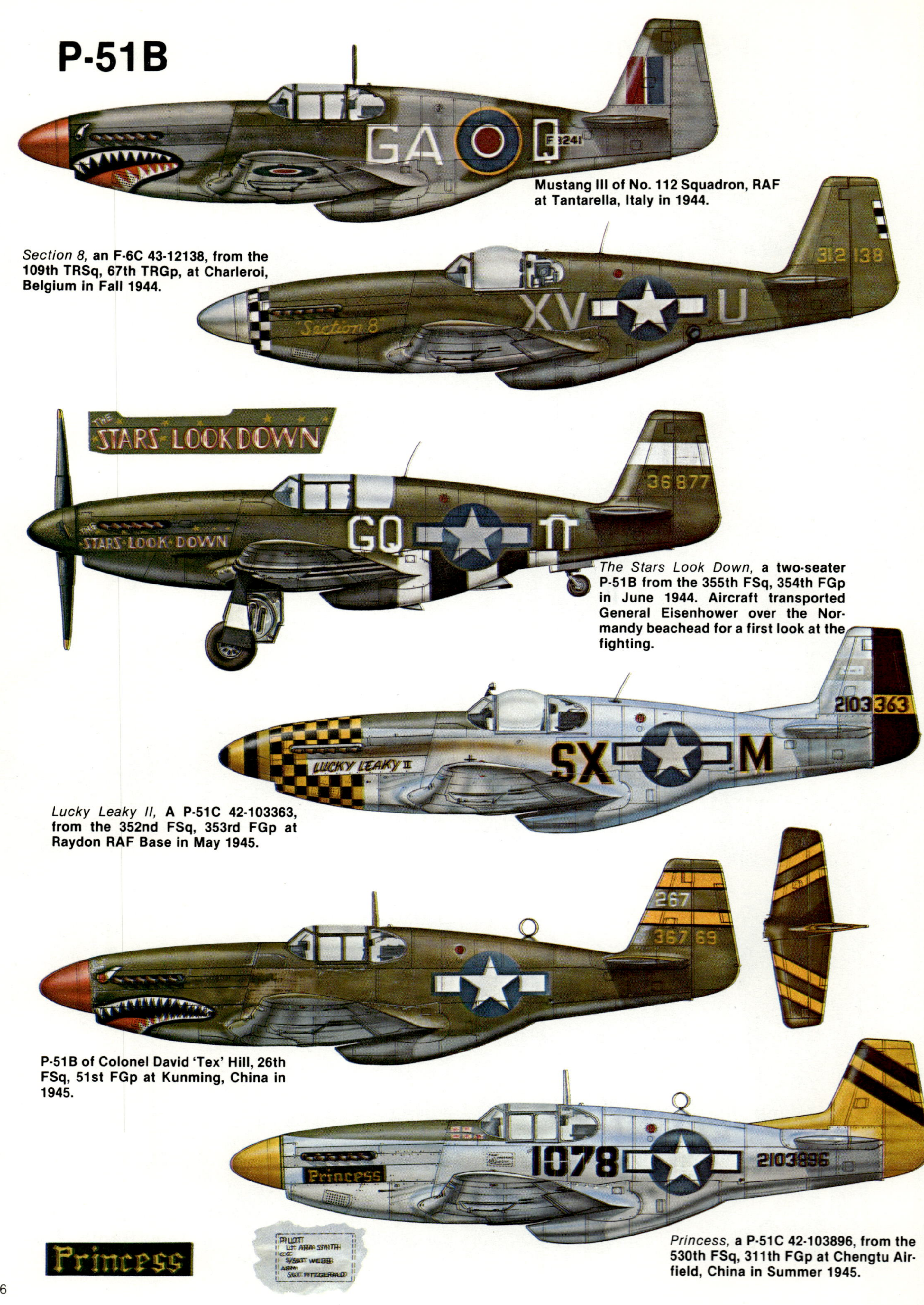

Mustang III of No. 112 Squadron, RAF at Tantarella, Italy in 1944.

Section 8, an F-6C 43-12138, from the 109th TRSq, 67th TRGp, at Charleroi, Belgium in Fall 1944.

The Stars Look Down, a two-seater P-51B from the 355th FSq, 354th FGp in June 1944. Aircraft transported General Eisenhower over the Normandy beachead for a first look at the fighting.

Lucky Leaky II, A P-51C 42-103363, from the 352nd FSq, 353rd FGp at Raydon RAF Base in May 1945.

P-51B of Colonel David 'Tex' Hill, 26th FSq, 51st FGp at Kunming, China in 1945.

Princess, a P-51C 42-103896, from the 530th FSq, 311th FGp at Chengtu Airfield, China in Summer 1945.

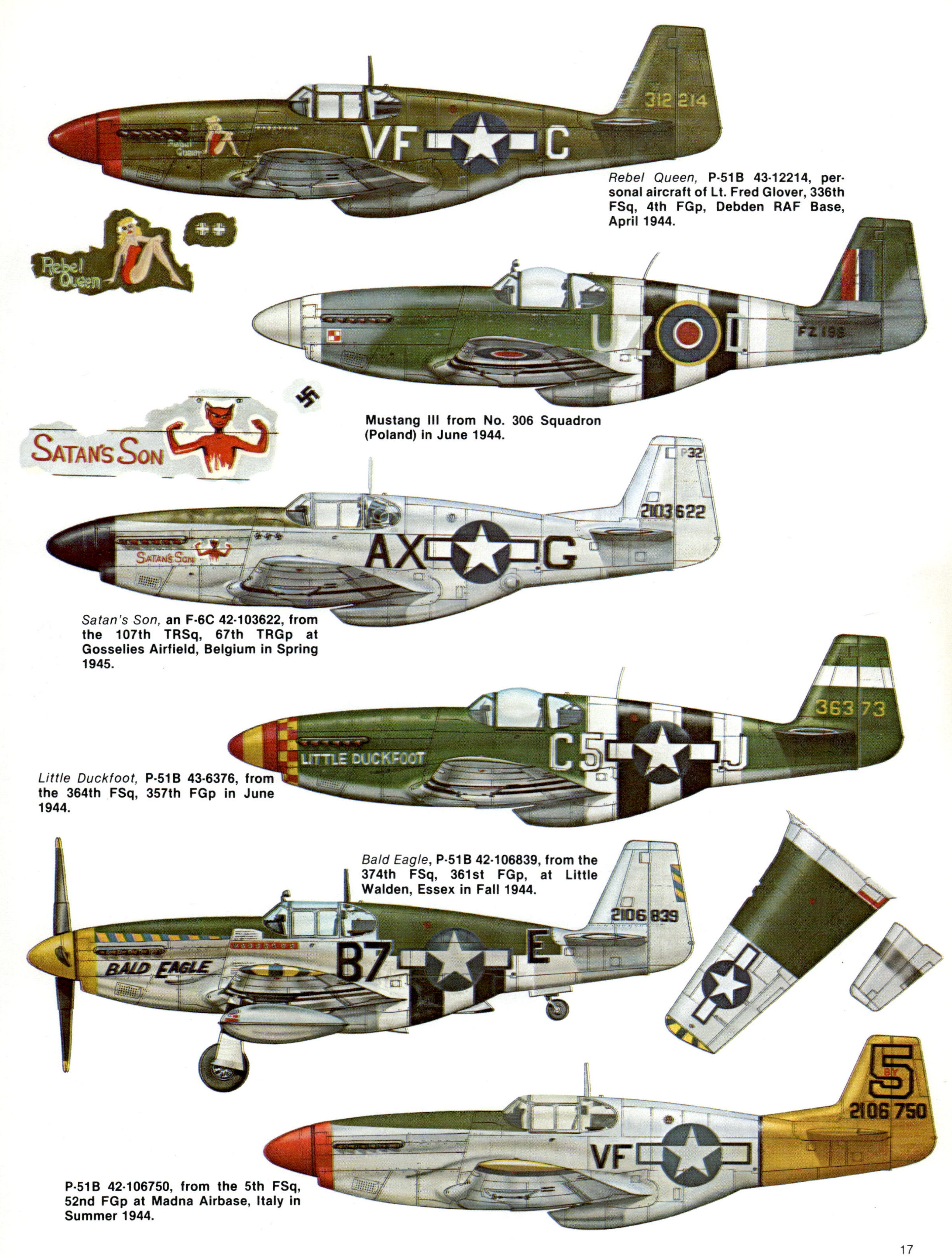

Rebel Queen, **P-51B 43-12214, personal aircraft of Lt. Fred Glover, 336th FSq, 4th FGp, Debden RAF Base, April 1944.**

Mustang III from No. 306 Squadron (Poland) in June 1944.

Satan's Son, **an F-6C 42-103622, from the 107th TRSq, 67th TRGp at Gosselies Airfield, Belgium in Spring 1945.**

Little Duckfoot, **P-51B 43-6376, from the 364th FSq, 357th FGp in June 1944.**

Bald Eagle, **P-51B 42-106839, from the 374th FSq, 361st FGp, at Little Walden, Essex in Fall 1944.**

P-51B 42-106750, from the 5th FSq, 52nd FGp at Madna Airbase, Italy in Summer 1944.

P-51D Mustang

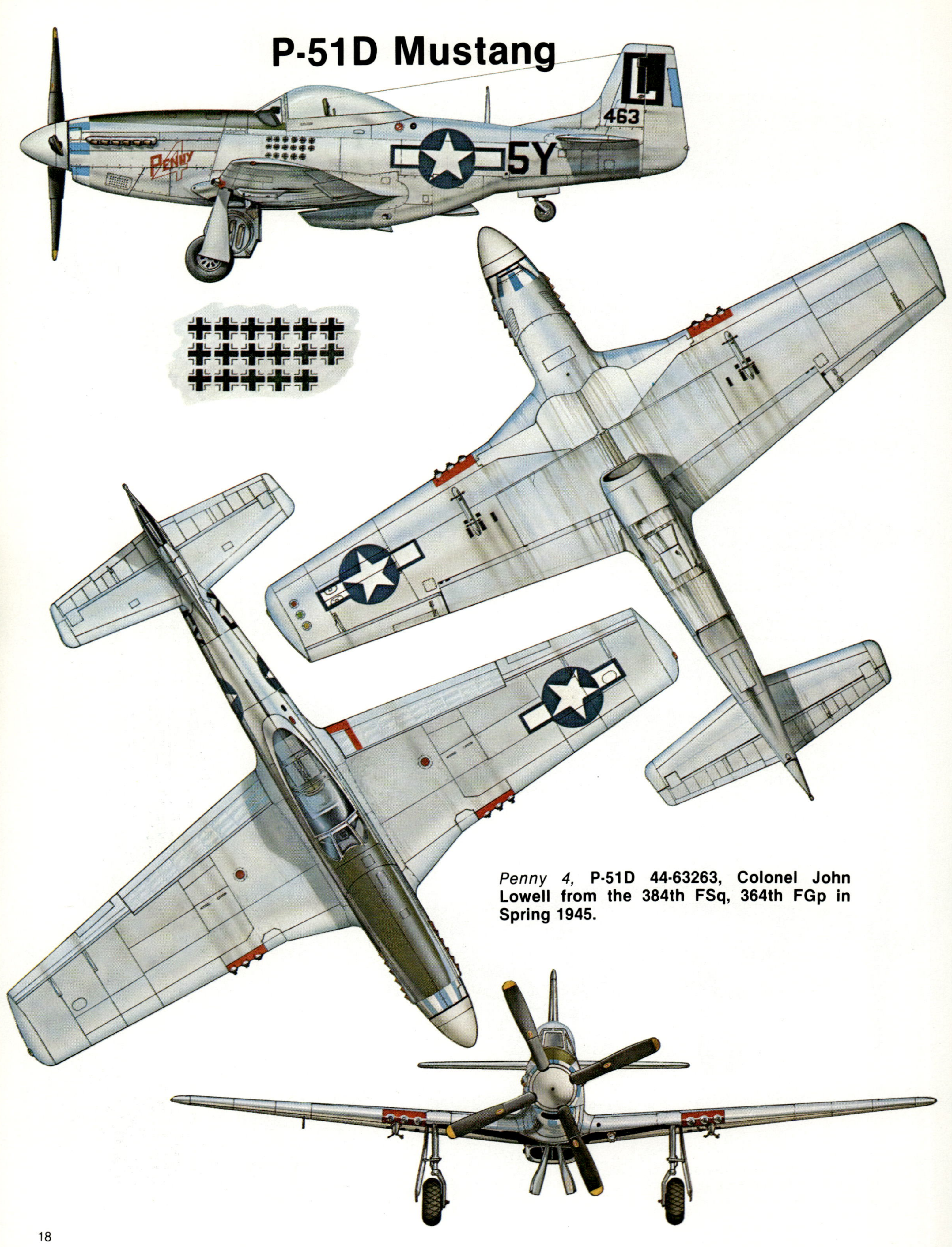

Penny 4, **P-51D 44-63263, Colonel John Lowell from the 384th FSq, 364th FGp in Spring 1945.**

P-51D Details

P-51D Cockpit, Canopy, Mirror, and Radio Gear

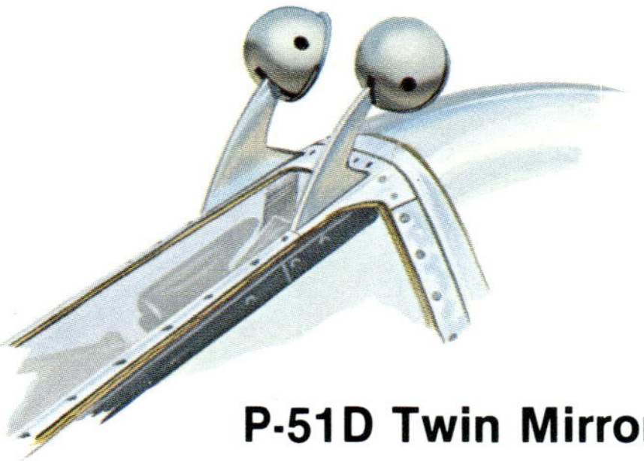

P-51D Twin Mirror

K-14A Gunsight

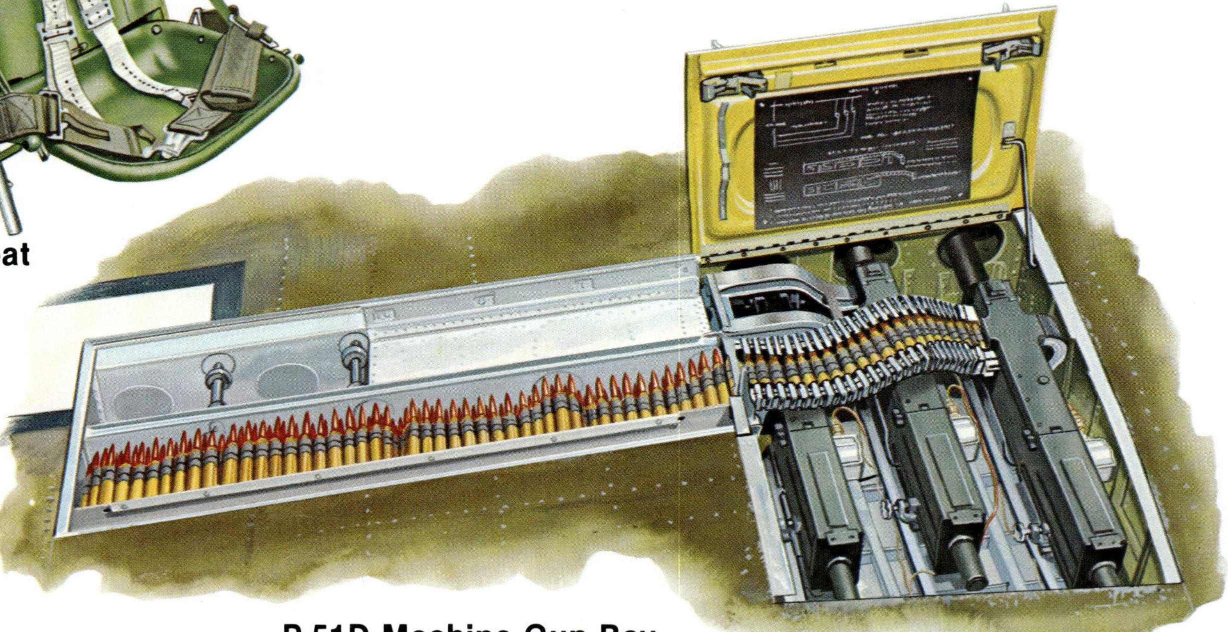

P-51D Seat

P-51D Machine Gun Bay

P-51D Details

P-51D

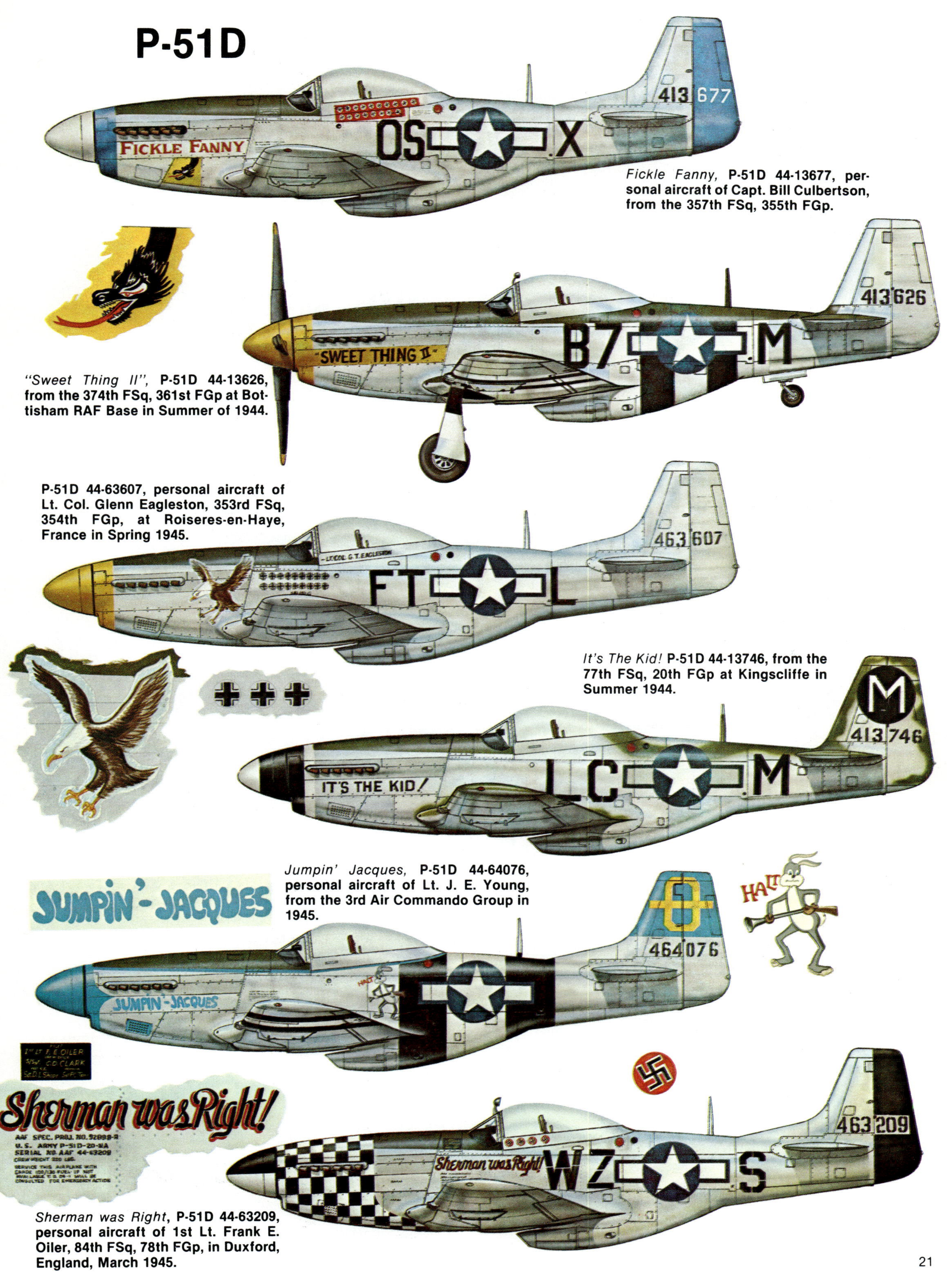

Fickle Fanny, **P-51D 44-13677, personal aircraft of Capt. Bill Culbertson, from the 357th FSq, 355th FGp.**

"Sweet Thing II", **P-51D 44-13626, from the 374th FSq, 361st FGp at Bottisham RAF Base in Summer of 1944.**

P-51D 44-63607, personal aircraft of Lt. Col. Glenn Eagleston, 353rd FSq, 354th FGp, at Roiseres-en-Haye, France in Spring 1945.

It's The Kid! **P-51D 44-13746, from the 77th FSq, 20th FGp at Kingscliffe in Summer 1944.**

Jumpin' Jacques, **P-51D 44-64076, personal aircraft of Lt. J. E. Young, from the 3rd Air Commando Group in 1945.**

Sherman was Right, **P-51D 44-63209, personal aircraft of 1st Lt. Frank E. Oiler, 84th FSq, 78th FGp, in Duxford, England, March 1945.**

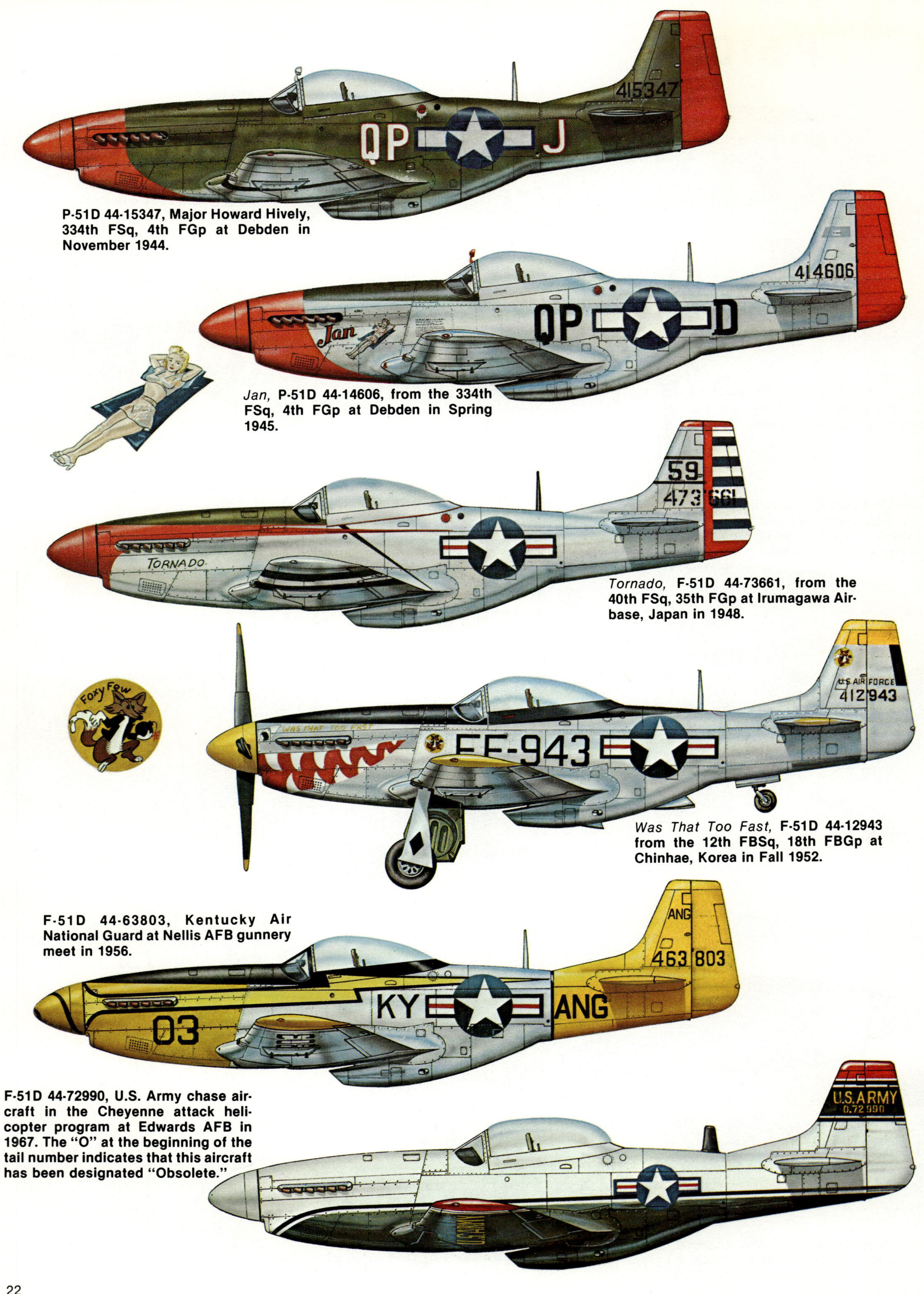

P-51D 44-15347, Major Howard Hively, 334th FSq, 4th FGp at Debden in November 1944.

Jan, P-51D 44-14606, from the 334th FSq, 4th FGp at Debden in Spring 1945.

Tornado, F-51D 44-73661, from the 40th FSq, 35th FGp at Irumagawa Air-base, Japan in 1948.

Was That Too Fast, F-51D 44-12943 from the 12th FBSq, 18th FBGp at Chinhae, Korea in Fall 1952.

F-51D 44-63803, Kentucky Air National Guard at Nellis AFB gunnery meet in 1956.

F-51D 44-72990, U.S. Army chase aircraft in the Cheyenne attack helicopter program at Edwards AFB in 1967. The "O" at the beginning of the tail number indicates that this aircraft has been designated "Obsolete."

F-82 Details

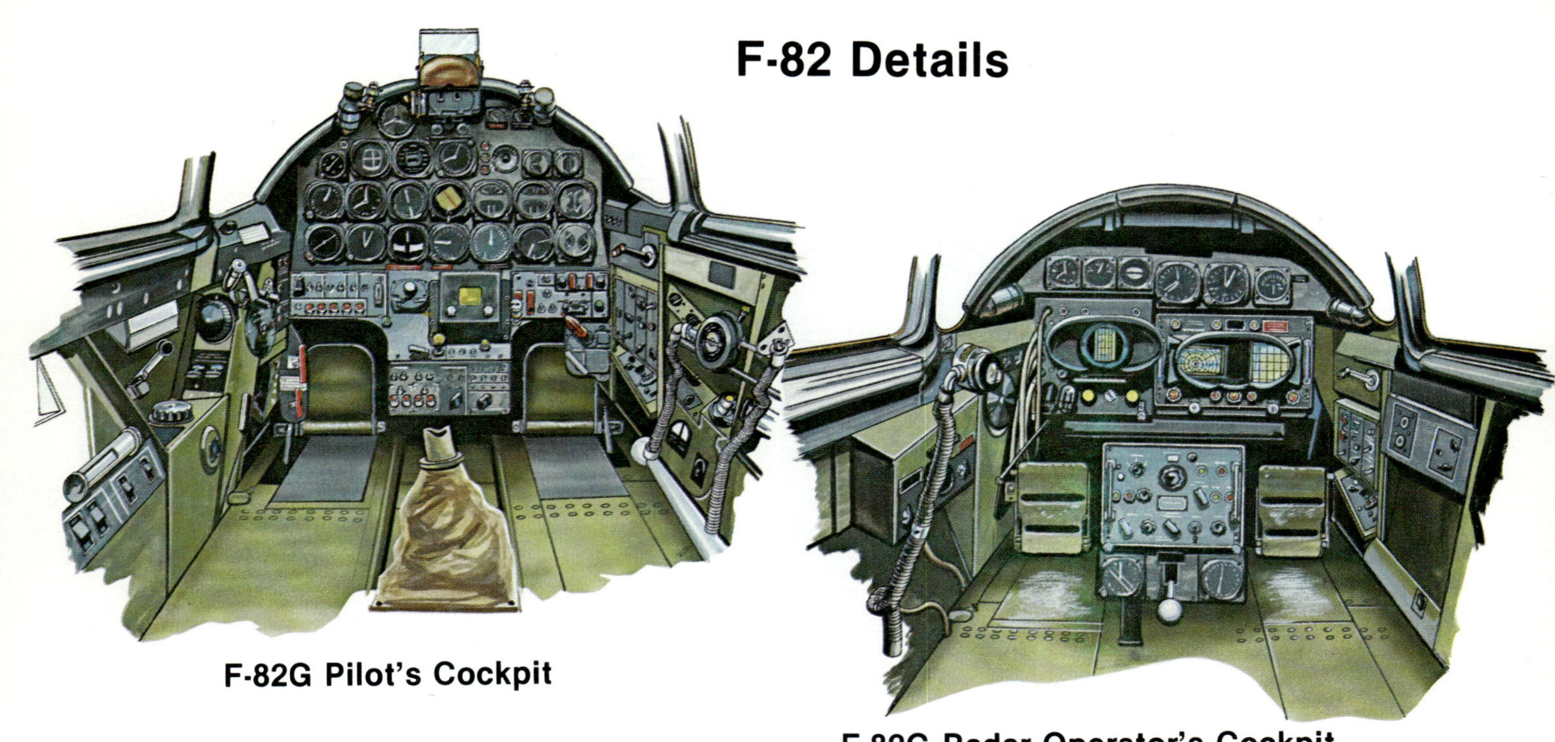

F-82G Pilot's Cockpit

F-82G Radar Operator's Cockpit

F-82 Rocket Launcher

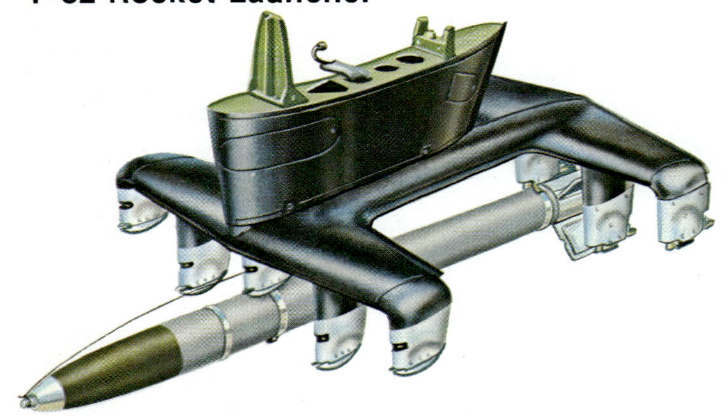

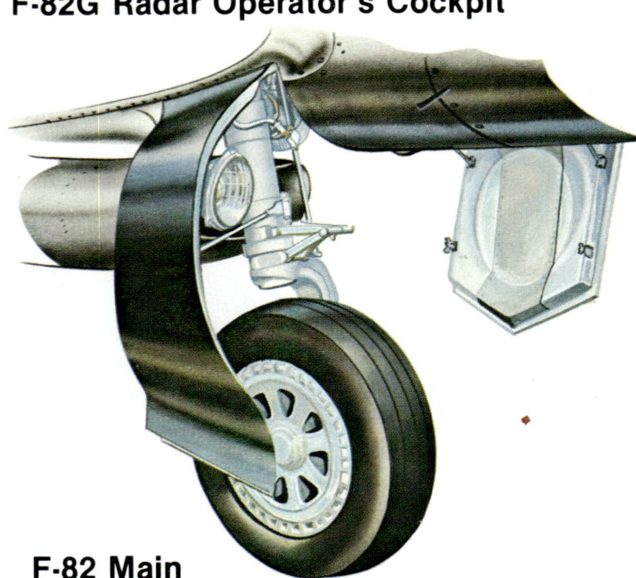

F-82 Main
Landing Gear Outer

F-82 Machine Gun Bay

F-82 Main
Landing Gear Inner

F-82

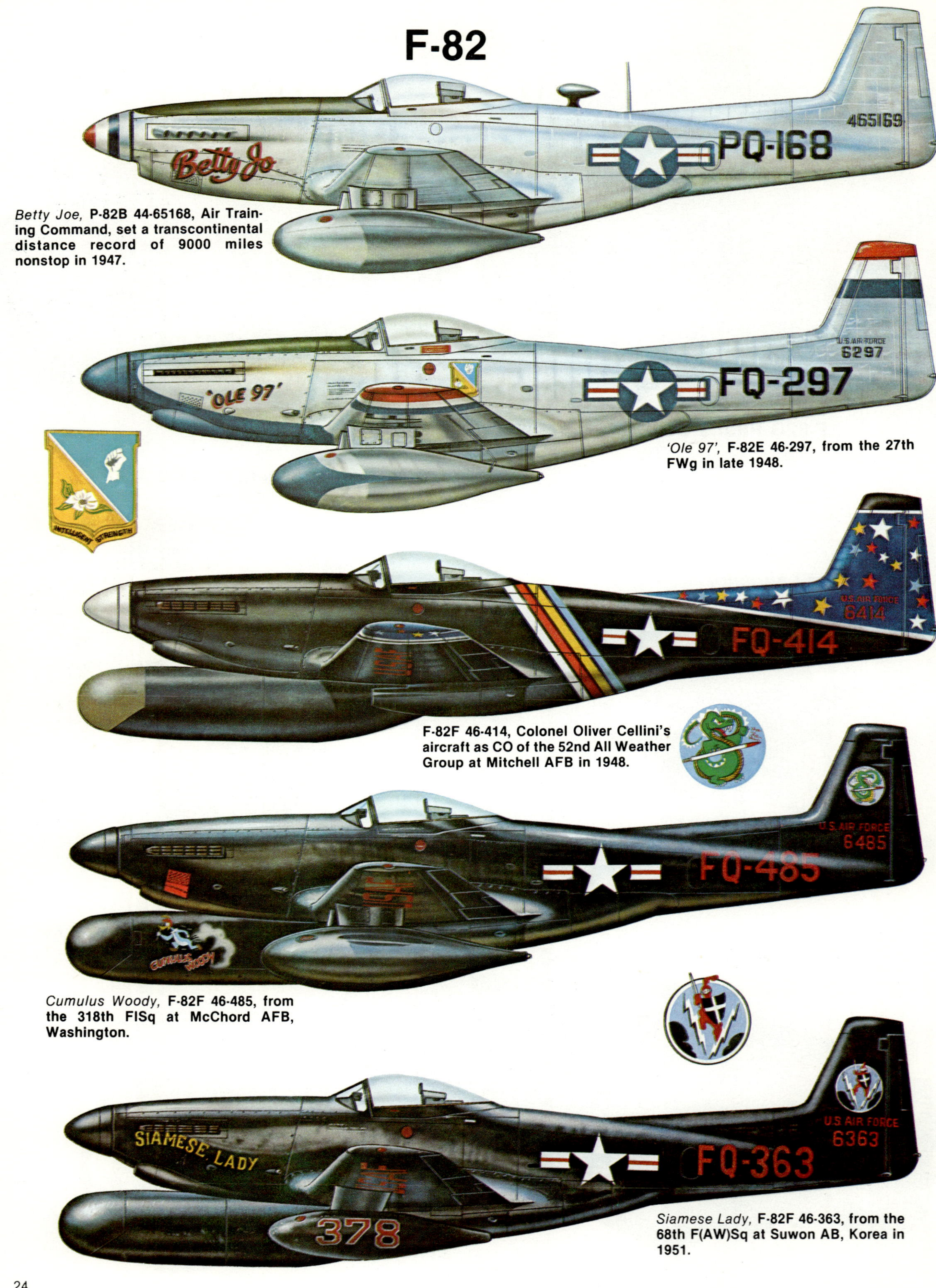

Betty Joe, **P-82B 44-65168, Air Training Command, set a transcontinental distance record of 9000 miles nonstop in 1947.**

'Ole 97', **F-82E 46-297, from the 27th FWg in late 1948.**

F-82F 46-414, Colonel Oliver Cellini's aircraft as CO of the 52nd All Weather Group at Mitchell AFB in 1948.

Cumulus Woody, **F-82F 46-485, from the 318th FISq at McChord AFB, Washington.**

Siamese Lady, **F-82F 46-363, from the 68th F(AW)Sq at Suwon AB, Korea in 1951.**

One of the most famous, and controversial Mustangs that ever flew was E2☆S from the 375th FSq/361st FGp. Many have thought that the 375th FSq camouflaged some of their aircraft with Insignia Blue paint instead of Olive Drab. However, E2☆S was flown by Captain Urban Drew, here during a publicity photo session on 11 July 1944. He since has stated, "the 361st FGp had no blue camouflage schemes." (USAF)

(Above) A flight of 353rd FGp P-51Ds sits on the ramp at Debach in the Fall of 1944. By this date only the underside of the fuselage retains the D-Day stripes, and these have been 'greyed-out' as has the national insignia. The normal home base for the 353rd was Raydon. (USAF)

Tika IV peels off to the right displaying the full D-Day stripes. Note how ragged and uneven the wing stripes are. The fuselage stripes have disappeared either through normal wear or from replacement panels. (USAF)

European Theater Mustangs wore some of the gaudiest unit paint schemes in aircraft history. *Sunny VIII* is Colonel Everett Stewart's personal mount and wears the late war 4th FGp markings of a red nose sweeping back under the wing leading edge, light blue anti-glare panel with red trim, and a light blue rudder. Note the dual mirrors on the windscreen. (Stewart via Mitchell)

(Below, Left & Right) Illustrating the many paint schemes that Mustangs carried is Major Clarence Anderson's *Old Crow* from the 363rd FSq/357th FGp. (Below Left) As she appeared in the Summer of 1944 with Medium Green (42) upper surfaces and Medium Sea Grey undersides. (Below) Six months later and camouflage is no longer needed. The spinner and nose checks are red and yellow, while the rudder is red with yellow numbers. (via Garrett)

In this author's opinion, the 78th FGp had the prettiest markings of all the Mustang units. *Contrary Mary* was the personal aircraft of Lt. Col. Roy Caviness, CO of the 78th FGp in the Summer of 1945. Black and white checkerboard on the nose, rudder, and upper and lower wingtips, with red trim. Aircraft name and unit codes are black with red outline; while the canopy frame is in yellow with fourteen black victory crosses. (USAF)

Penny 4 and Colonel John Lowell, CO of the 364th FGp. White spinner, blue and white striped nose are 364th FGp markings. The name is in red as is the panel surrounding the guns. Codes were 5Y aft of the star and bar, and a white L (for Lowell) on a black square on the vertical tail. The complete serial was 44-63263 but only the 463 was carried on the port side and 263 on the starboard side. Note the Hamilton Standard emblem on each prop blade. (via Garrett)

(Below) A P-51K Mustang IV from No. 3 Squadron, Royal Australian Air Force. Allied Forces, non-US, Mustangs carried full camouflage well into 1945 before going to the natural metal scheme that USAAF P-51s had been using since Spring 1944. It was after Operation Big Week, in February 1944, that US planners declared air superiority over the Continent. (Smith via Ethell)

(Above) Major W.B. Bailey, his ground crew, and *Double Trouble Two,* pose for the camera at Raydon RAF airbase. The 353rd FGp outlined their unit code letters with yellow to match their black and yellow checkerboard noses. (USAF)

(Below) A flight of No. 3 Squadron, RAAF, Mustang IVs over Italy in 1945; three are in natural metal and the fourth is in the Dark Green/Ocean Grey camouflage. Note that Mustang IVs had louvered vent panels on the nose in place of the holes common on USAAF P-51s. (Smith via Ethell)

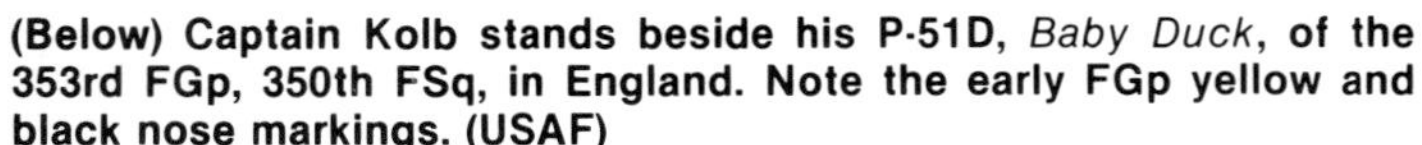
(Below) Captain Kolb stands beside his P-51D, *Baby Duck*, of the 353rd FGp, 350th FSq, in England. Note the early FGp yellow and black nose markings. (USAF)

Lt. Colonel Joe Thury was credited with 25½ ground kills in *Pauline*, 6N ☆ C #44-14656. Her spinner and nose checks are red and white for the 339th FGp, the rudder is yellow for the 504th FSq. The small cross on the fuselage indicates that the aircraft has had a fuselage fuel tank installed. (USAF)

Sometimes aircraft names told a story. Obviously the pilot of this 41st FSq, 35th FGp P-51D had a girl at home who broke her promise to wait. Many Pacific-based units reverted back to the pre-war practice of painting the rudder with red, white, and blue stripes. The black and white fuselage and wing bands were used after the Philippine Islands invasion for easy recognition by friendly forces. (LePage via Johnson)

Tiny Gay Babe and *Three of a Kind* from the 46th FSq, 21st FGp on Iwo Jima in 1945, with Mt. Surabachi in the background. Spinner, tail stripe, and wing and stabilizer tips are Medium Blue with Black trim. *Three of a Kind* refers to the aircraft serial number, 44-63777 — a natural! (USAF)

Mustangs continued on active duty with US Air Force units well into the 1950s. This element, a F-51D and a F-6D, from the 37th FISq.,carried a blue band with white stars and trim around the nose which was repeated on the tail. The spinner is halved in blue and white, while the wingtips are blue. The antiglare panel is black. Note the different antenna styles. (USAF via Isham)

Dooleybird, **a Mustang IV from No. 19 Squadron, RAF, in 1945. Many areas of RAF 'natural metal' Mustangs were actually painted silver. Nose checks, spinner tip, canopy bottom, and trim to the antiglare panel is Medium Blue. The name is red with black trim. Code letters QV-V, and serial KM 272 are black. (Flt. Lt. A.S. Doley via R.L. Ward)**

Mustangs returned to combat in 1950 over the Korean peninsula. These aircraft are from the 12th Fighter Bomber Squadron. The large underwing tanks are napalm. In the Korean War, Mustangs were used mainly in the close air support and ResCAP role. However, they did escort B-29s to North Korean targets on many occasions, a role with which they were quite familiar. (USAF)

Major James Miller taxis in at Wright Field, site of the Air Force Museum, with the last F-51 in Air Force service. The date is 27 January 1957. The last unit she served with was the West Virginia Air National Guard. The Air National Guard was extensively equipped with F-51s during the jet-transition era of the early 1950s. (USAF)

In the late 1960s, the P-51 Mustang came back into the US Army, this time as a chase aircraft in the Cheyenne attack helicopter program. The upper fuselage was white, with the wings and lower fuselage in Olive Drab - but glossy. The trim line was black, while the tailtip and wingtips were red. (NAA)

One of several P-51Ds exported to the Dominican Republic under the Military Assistance Program. The aircraft is painted overall grey for corrosion control. This aircraft was captured by elements of the 82nd Airborne Division during the Dominican Crisis of 1965. (USAF)

Oh! Marie, an F-51H from the 64th FSq at Elmendorf AFB, Alaska in 1947. The career of the F-51H was very short in active Air Force units due to the great influx of jet aircraft. However, they soldiered on with many Air Guard units until the mid-1950s. (AFM)

(Above) The F-51Hs were in service with active US Air Force units the least amount of time of any Mustang type. They were an excellent aircraft but were phased out to make room for the new all-jet Air Force. These aircraft are from the 112th FBWg, Pennsylvania Air Guard. 259 is an ex-New York ANG aircraft and still carries its colors. (USAF)

The crew chief of this California Air Guard F-51H watches as the Sabre Knights F-86D team performs. Note the twin antennas, underwing rocket rails, and typical P-51 exhaust staining. Air Guard aircraft carried ANG and the last three digits of the serial on both the upper right and lower left wing, in place of USAF. (NAA)

(Above) An F-82H from the 449th FISq at Elmendorf AFB, Alaska. The tail and outer wing panels are painted Arctic Red for higher visibility in case the aircraft was forced down in the snow covered countryside. All US Air Force non-camouflaged aircraft that fly over, or through, Canadian or Arctic areas are painted in this manner. (AFM)

(Above and Right) *Cumulus Woody*, an F-82F from the 318th FISq at McChord AFB, Washington. Most of the F-82 units allowed some type of artwork on their aircraft. The F-82F/G radar pod was a natural for the unit artists to ply their trades on. (Menard)

(Left) Exhibition of the typical finish of an operational all black night fighter F-82F/G. Note the well worn antiglare panels and the blotchy effect on the leading edges of the wings caused by touching up the paint. (AFM)